SQL
Made Easy

*Tips and Tricks to Mastering SQL
Programming*

Ryan Campbell

Table of Contents

Introduction 12

The Importance of SQL in Modern Programming.................14

Setting the Stage for Learning SQL Efficiently.....................17

Chapter 1: SQL Fundamentals Recap.................. 20

Brief Overview of SQL Basics 20

Queries: Unleashing the Power 20

Basic Query Structure 21

Examples of Basic Queries 22

Understanding Data Types 22

A Preview of Data Manipulation 23

Understanding Database Structures...........................23

Tables: Building Blocks of Databases 23

Primary Keys: The Identifiers 24

Foreign Keys: Building Relationships..........................24

Views: Customized Perspectives 25

Stored Procedures and Functions: Reusable Code 25

SQL Syntax Refresher 26

Keywords and Commands 26

Clauses and Statements.. 27

Comments.. 28

String Literals 28

Wildcard Characters 29

Chapter 2: Essential Data Manipulation Techniques 31

SELECT Statements and Filtering Data................... 31

Filtering Data with the WHERE Clause 32

Combining Conditions 33

Grouping Data with GROUP BY............................. 35

Aggregation Functions for Data Analysis 37

SUM: Adding Values 37

AVG: Finding Averages 38

GROUP BY with Aggregation Functions 38

Chapter 3: Joining and Combining Data 41

Inner Joins: Bridging Related Data........................ 41

Outer Joins: Including Non-Matching Data 42

Right Outer Join 42

Left and Right Joins in One Example 43

Full Outer Joins: Comprehensive Matching 44

Cross Joins and Self-Joins...44

Cross Joins: Exploring All Combinations 45

Self-Joins: Unveiling Intra-Table Relationships..........46

Combining Techniques for Advanced Insights 46

Chapter 4: Advanced Query Optimization 48

Indexing and its Impact on Performance 48

The Role of Indexes 48

Types of Indexes..48

Creating Indexes..49

Impact on Performance 49

Monitoring and Maintaining Indexes.........................50

Subqueries and their Practical Applications 51

Understanding Subqueries...51

Common Table Expressions (CTEs) for Enhanced Readability
....54

Benefits of Using CTEs 55

Practical Applications of CTEs...56

Example of Using CTEs..56

Mastering CTEs for Clearer Queries 57

Chapter 5: Working with Complex Data Types ...58

Handling Dates, Times, and Time Zones...............................58

Understanding Date and Time Data Types 58

Time Zones and Timestamps 59

Dealing with Daylight Saving Time 59

Practical Applications...60

Example: Handling Time Zones...60

Mastering Time Manipulation 61

Dealing with Strings and Textual Data 61

Manipulating Textual Data..62

Pattern Matching with LIKE and Regular Expressions 62

Concatenating and Formatting Strings 62

Practical Applications...63

Example: Extracting Initials..63

Harnessing the Power of Strings 64

Storing and Retrieving Binary Data 64

Binary Data Types 64

Storing Binary Data 65

Retrieving Binary Data 65

Harnessing the Flexibility of Binary Data 67

Chapter 6: Managing Databases and Tables 68

Creating, Modifying, and Deleting Databases 68

Creating Databases 68

Modifying Databases 69

Deleting Databases 69

Backup and Restore 69

Practical Applications 70

Example: Creating a Database 70

Mastering Database Management 71

Constraints and Data Integrity 74

Types of Constraints 74

Importance of Constraints 75

Safeguarding Your Data with Constraints 77

Chapter 7: Stored Procedures and Functions 79

Creating and Executing Stored Procedures 79

Stored Procedures 79

Functions 80

Empowering Code Organization 83

User-Defined Functions for Custom Operations................. 83

Creating User-Defined Functions... 83

Using User-Defined Functions 84

Advantages of User-Defined Functions 84

Custom Functions, Powerful Queries 85

Benefits of Using Procedural SQL 86

Enriching Data Management 89

Chapter 8: Advanced Data Analysis with Window Functions...90

Understanding Window Functions and Their Usage 90

Ranking, Row Numbering, and Percentile Calculations 90

Moving Averages and Rolling Aggregations 91

Unveiling Insights with Window Functions............................92

Chapter 9: Securing Your SQL Environment 95

Role-Based Access Control..95

Defining Roles and Permissions 95

Encrypting Data and Protecting Sensitive Information..........96

Preventing SQL Injection Attacks 97

Practical Implementation and Beyond.....................................98

Fortifying Your SQL Environment 99

Chapter 10: Working with External Data Sources

.... 100

Importing and Exporting Data...100

Integrating SQL with NoSQL and Web Services 101

Connecting to APIs and External APIs...................................102

Pushing Boundaries in Data Integration 103

Data Fusion Maestro..104

Chapter 11: Real-World Application Scenarios .105

Building Reports and Dashboards with SQL 105

E-Commerce Inventory Management System 106

Healthcare Patient Records System 107

Educational Institution Management System 108

Elevating Solutions with SQL Prowess 109

Applying SQL to Marketing and Customer Analysis 109

Customer Segmentation 110

Campaign Effectiveness Assessment 110

Churn Prediction and Retention Strategies 111

Customer Lifetime Value Analysis 112

Seizing Marketing Opportunities with SQL 112

Chapter 12: Future Trends in SQL Programming

....114

Exploring New SQL Features and Enhancements 114

Window Functions: Unleashing Analytical Power 114

Common Table Expressions (CTEs): Enhanced Readability . 115

JSON Functions: Handling Unstructured Data 116

Temporal Data: Navigating Time Travel 116

Machine Learning Integration: Bridging SQL and AI 117

Embracing the SQL Frontier 117

Integration with Machine Learning and AI: Unleashing Data Superpowers 118

A Glimpse of the Future: Predictive Analytics with SQL 118

From Raw Data to AI-Ready: Data Preprocessing 119

In-Database Predictions: Streamlined Insights 119

Scalability and Beyond: SQL + AI Collaboration 120

Mastering the Fusion for Data Superpowers 120

The Evolving Role of SQL in Data-Driven Decision Making ..121

From Querying to Insight: SQL's Evolution 121

SQL Meets Advanced Analytics: The Synergy 122

Decision-Driving Power: SQL and Real-Time Analytics 124

SQL for All: Democratizing Data Insights............................124

SQL's Renaissance in Decision Making 125

Conclusion 127

Navigating Your SQL Odyssey...127

Reflecting on Your SQL Journey 127

Encouragement to Continue Exploring and Learning SQL...128

Appendix: Additional Resources 130

Recommended Books, Online Courses, and Tutorials 130

SQL Cheat Sheets and Quick References 131

Online Communities and Forums for SQL Enthusiasts 131

Introduction

Welcome to "SQL Made Easy: Tips and Tricks to Mastering SQL Programming." Are you ready to embark on a journey that will unlock the power of SQL and revolutionize your programming skills? Whether you're a beginner taking your first steps into the world of databases or an experienced developer seeking to refine your SQL prowess, this book is your ultimate guide.

In today's data-driven landscape, SQL is the cornerstone of effective data management and analysis. From startups to multinational corporations, from web applications to mobile apps, the ability to harness the capabilities of SQL sets you on a path to success. And that's precisely where this book comes in.

Imagine writing complex queries with confidence, seamlessly joining and transforming data, and creating reports that empower your decision-making. Picture yourself navigating databases with the finesse of a seasoned pro, optimizing your code for peak performance, and safeguarding your systems against vulnerabilities. With "SQL Made Easy," these goals are well within your reach.

Our journey through these pages will take you from foundational SQL concepts to advanced techniques that will elevate your coding game. We'll delve into the intricacies of data manipulation, guide you through the art of crafting efficient queries, and unveil the secrets of designing robust databases. Along the way, we'll share practical examples, insider tips, and real-world scenarios that illustrate the true potential of SQL.

But this book isn't just about mastering syntax; it's about empowering you to wield SQL as a tool of transformation. Whether you're an analyst, a programmer, a data scientist, or anyone in between, the knowledge you gain from these pages will open doors to new opportunities and possibilities.

So, why choose "SQL Made Easy"? Because this isn't just another technical manual—it's your gateway to becoming a SQL maestro. As you turn the pages and embark on this learning journey, remember that you're not alone. The vast and dynamic world of SQL programming awaits, and this book is your compass. Buckle up, dear reader, as we navigate through the exciting realms of SQL programming and equip you with the skills to master it like never before.

Your journey starts now. Let's dive in!

The Importance of SQL in Modern Programming

In the fast-paced digital age, where data is the currency that fuels innovation and decision-making, SQL emerges as a foundational pillar of modern programming. As applications become more complex and data volumes explode, the ability to efficiently manage, retrieve, and manipulate data is no longer a luxury—it's a necessity.

Structured Query Language (SQL), often referred to as the language of databases, serves as the bridge between raw data and actionable insights. Whether you're working on a website, a mobile app, an e-commerce platform, or a sophisticated data analytics project, SQL underpins your ability to access, organize, and utilize data effectively.

In a world where information resides in sprawling databases and intricate data systems, SQL offers several critical advantages:

1. Data Retrieval and Manipulation

SQL empowers you to retrieve specific subsets of data from vast databases with precision. Whether you're fetching records for a user's account details or searching for specific transactions within a dataset, SQL's querying power ensures that you get the information you need swiftly and accurately.

2. Seamless Data Integration

Modern applications rarely exist in isolation. They interact with various data sources and external APIs, necessitating seamless data integration. SQL excels at merging, joining, and combining data from different tables and databases, providing a cohesive view of information from diverse origins.

3. Efficient Data Aggregation

From calculating averages and sums to determining the highest and lowest values, SQL's aggregate functions simplify the process of extracting valuable insights from data. Whether you're analyzing sales trends or summarizing user behaviors, these functions are indispensable tools.

4. Data Integrity and Security

Maintaining data integrity and ensuring security are paramount concerns. SQL's robust features for enforcing constraints, such as unique keys and foreign keys, prevent data anomalies and inconsistencies. Additionally, SQL offers mechanisms for controlling user access and protecting sensitive information.

5. Scalability and Performance Optimization

As applications scale and user bases grow, maintaining performance becomes critical. SQL's ability to optimize queries and utilize indexing ensures that database operations remain efficient, even as datasets expand.

6. Informed Decision-Making

In the era of data-driven decision-making, SQL empowers businesses to extract actionable insights from their data. By querying and analyzing historical trends, user behavior, and market patterns, SQL enables informed strategies and smarter choices.

In "SQL Made Easy: Tips and Tricks to Mastering SQL Programming," we delve into these aspects and beyond, equipping you with the knowledge and skills to navigate the world of modern programming with confidence. Whether you're a developer, an analyst, or a business professional seeking to harness the power of data, the journey you're about to embark upon will empower you.

Setting the Stage for Learning SQL Efficiently

Embarking on the journey to master SQL programming is an exciting endeavor—one that promises to unlock a realm of data manipulation and analysis possibilities. To make the most of this journey, it's essential to lay a strong foundation that will support your learning and growth in the world of SQL.

The Mindset of a Learner

Approach this journey with the mindset of a curious and determined learner. SQL, like any programming language, requires practice and exploration. Embrace the challenges as opportunities to deepen your understanding and sharpen your skills.

A Comfortable Learning Environment

Create a comfortable and focused environment for your learning. Ensure you have access to a computer or device where you can interact with databases and practice SQL queries.

Resources at Your Fingertips

Utilize the resources available to you. Apart from this book, there are a plethora of online tutorials, forums, and courses that can supplement your learning. Bookmark useful websites, download helpful cheat sheets, and engage with online communities where you can seek guidance and share your insights.

Hands-On Practice

The heart of mastering SQL lies in hands-on practice. Don't just read about concepts—implement them. Experiment with SQL queries, create sample databases, and challenge yourself with real-world scenarios. The more you practice, the more confident you'll become in writing and understanding SQL code.

A Growth-Oriented Mindset

Every challenge you overcome and every query you master brings you closer to SQL proficiency. Approach setbacks as opportunities for growth.

Stay Curious and Creative

SQL is a versatile tool with numerous applications. As you learn, consider how you can creatively apply SQL to solve real-world problems. Think beyond the examples you encounter, and explore how SQL can contribute to your specific field or interests.

Patience and Persistence

Becoming proficient in SQL takes time and dedication. Don't rush the process. Persistence is key; even complex concepts can be mastered with dedication and consistent effort.

As we embark on this journey through "SQL Made Easy: Tips and Tricks to Mastering SQL Programming," keep these principles in mind. Each chapter is designed to build upon the knowledge you've gained, guiding you through progressively more advanced techniques. With the right mindset and an eagerness to learn, you're well on your way to becoming a SQL programming expert. So, let's dive in and lay the groundwork for an enriching and rewarding learning experience.

Chapter 1: SQL Fundamentals Recap

Brief Overview of SQL Basics

Before we dive into the intricate world of SQL programming, let's start by building a solid understanding of the fundamental concepts that underpin this language. SQL, or Structured Query Language, serves as a means of communicating with relational databases. It's the language through which we interact with data, perform operations, and retrieve valuable insights.

Relational Databases: The Foundation

At the core of SQL is the concept of a relational database. Imagine a structured collection of data tables, where each table consists of rows (records) and columns (fields). These tables are interlinked through relationships, forming a robust framework for organizing and managing data.

Queries: Unleashing the Power

At its heart, SQL is a querying language. A query is a command that instructs the database to retrieve, manipulate, or perform an action on data. It's akin to asking a question—the database responds with the relevant information. Queries can be as simple as retrieving a list of names or as complex as generating detailed analytical reports.

Basic Query Structure

A typical SQL query comprises distinct clauses:

- **SELECT**: Indicates the segments to recover from a table.

- **FROM**: Identifies the table from which data is being retrieved.

- **WHERE**: Channels information in view of determined conditions.

- **BUNCH BY**: Gatherings information in view of a particular segment.

- **HAVING**: Filters grouped data further based on conditions.

- **REQUEST BY**: Sorts the outcome set in light of determined segments.

- **LIMIT/OFFSET**: Restricts the number of rows returned (for pagination).

Examples of Basic Queries

Here are a couple of simple SQL queries to illustrate its basic structure:

1. Retrieve all customer names from the "Customers" table:

SQL Copy code

```sql
SELECT customer_name FROM Customers;
```

2. Retrieve orders with a total amount greater than $100 from the "Orders" table:

SQL Copy code

```sql
SELECT * FROM Orders WHERE total_amount > 100;
```

Understanding Data Types

SQL handles a variety of data types, such as integers, strings, dates, and more. These data types define the kind of information a column can hold, ensuring data accuracy and consistency.

A Preview of Data Manipulation

SQL not only retrieves data but also allows you to modify and insert data. You can update existing records, delete unwanted data, and insert new records into tables.

As we journey deeper into SQL programming, these fundamental concepts will serve as the bedrock of your knowledge. Armed with this understanding, we'll progress to more complex queries, join operations, and advanced techniques. The world of SQL programming awaits, and armed with the basics, you're ready to explore its intricacies and possibilities.

Understanding Database Structures

To navigate the realm of SQL programming effectively, it's essential to grasp the fundamental structure that underlies relational databases. Databases are like organized repositories that store data in a structured manner, allowing efficient data retrieval, manipulation, and management.

Tables: Building Blocks of Databases

At the core of a relational database are tables. Tables consist of rows and columns, creating a grid-like structure that resembles a spreadsheet. Each row represents a single record, while each column represents a specific attribute or property associated with the data.

Primary Keys: The Identifiers

Every table requires a primary key—an attribute that uniquely identifies each record. It ensures that each entry in the table is distinct and identifiable. Common examples of primary keys include customer IDs, order numbers, or ISBNs for books.

Foreign Keys: Building Relationships

In a relational database, tables are rarely isolated entities. They're often linked through relationships. A foreign key is a column in one table that refers to the primary key in another table, creating a connection between the two. These connections enable the establishment of complex relationships and the retrieval of data from multiple tables.

Normalization: Organizing Data Efficiently

Normalization is a technique used to organize data efficiently and reduce redundancy. By breaking down large tables into smaller, related tables, you maintain data integrity and prevent inconsistencies. This process streamlines data management and makes the database more robust.

Indexes: Speeding Up Queries

Imagine an index in a book that lists keywords and page numbers—indexes in databases work similarly. They enhance query performance by creating a quick reference to specific data points. Indexes are crucial for speeding up searches and ensuring that queries run efficiently, especially in large datasets.

Views: Customized Perspectives

Views provide customized perspectives of data without altering the underlying data itself. They're essentially saved queries that allow you to retrieve specific columns or filtered data from one or more tables. Views are handy for presenting relevant information to users without exposing the entire database structure.

Stored Procedures and Functions: Reusable Code

Stored procedures and functions are pre-written SQL code that can be stored and executed within the database. They promote code reusability, enhance security by limiting direct access to tables, and improve performance by reducing network traffic.

Triggers: Automated Actions

Triggers are automated responses to specific events. They can execute a set of actions whenever a certain condition is met. For instance, you can use triggers to update a timestamp whenever a new record is inserted or enforce business rules upon data changes.

Understanding these foundational elements of database structures is crucial as we delve further into SQL programming. By comprehending how data is organized and related within databases, you'll be better equipped to create efficient queries, design robust databases, and harness the true potential of SQL.

SQL Syntax Refresher

As we venture deeper into the world of SQL programming, let's revisit the syntax—the set of rules that govern how SQL commands are structured. SQL syntax provides the blueprint for crafting queries and interacting with databases effectively. Whether you're a newcomer or looking to refresh your memory, let's delve into the core components of SQL syntax.

Keywords and Commands

SQL commands are composed of keywords—reserved words with specific meanings in SQL. These keywords are not case-sensitive, but conventionally, they're written in uppercase for clarity. Some essential SQL commands include:

- **JOIN**: Combines data from multiple tables.

- **GROUP BY**: Groups data for aggregate functions.

- **ORDER BY**: Sorts the result set.

- **LIMIT/OFFSET**: Restricts the number of rows returned.

Clauses and Statements

SQL statements are composed of various clauses that collectively form a query. Here's a basic breakdown:

SQL Copy code

```sql
SELECT column1, column2
FROM table_name
WHERE condition
GROUP BY column1
HAVING condition
ORDER BY column1;
```

- The **FROM** clause indicates the table(s) from which data is retrieved.

- The **GROUP BY** clause groups data for aggregate functions.

- The **HAVING** clause filters grouped data based on conditions.

Comments

In SQL, comments help you annotate your code for clarity. Single-line comments start with two dashes (--), while multi-line comments are enclosed within /* ... */.

SQL Copy code

```
-- This is a single-line comment

/*
    This is a
    multi-line comment
*/
```

String Literals

String literals are enclosed within single quotes ('). They're used to represent textual values.

SQL Copy code

```
SELECT first_name, last_name
FROM employees
WHERE department = 'Marketing';
```

Wildcard Characters

Wildcard characters are used to match patterns within data.

SQL Copy code

```
SELECT product_name
FROM products
WHERE product_name LIKE 'App%';
```

Semicolon Termination

Most SQL statements are terminated with a semicolon (;). It's a best practice to end each SQL statement with a semicolon to ensure proper execution.

SQL Copy code

```
SELECT customer_name FROM customers;
```

As you reacquaint yourself with these fundamental elements of SQL syntax, you'll lay a strong foundation for the queries and operations we'll explore in the chapters ahead. This syntax refresher will serve as a valuable guide as we navigate through increasingly complex SQL commands and techniques.

Chapter 2: Essential Data Manipulation Techniques

SELECT Statements and Filtering Data

At the heart of SQL lies the power to retrieve and manipulate data using the **SELECT** statement. This fundamental command forms the basis for querying databases and extracting the information you need. Let's dive into the nuances of the **SELECT** statement and explore how to filter data effectively.

The basic structure of a **SELECT** statement is as follows:

SQL Copy code

```
SELECT column1, column2, ... FROM table_name;
```

- The **SELECT** keyword indicates that you're retrieving data.

- You specify the columns you want to retrieve after the **SELECT** keyword.

- The **FROM** keyword specifies the table from which you're retrieving the data.

For instance, to retrieve the names of all employees from the "employees" table, you'd use the following query:

SQL Copy code

```
SELECT first_name, last_name
FROM employees;
```

Filtering Data with the WHERE Clause

While retrieving all data from a table is useful, more often than not, you'll need to filter and retrieve specific subsets of data based on certain conditions.

The **WHERE** clause allows you to specify conditions that the retrieved data must meet. For instance, consider the following query that retrieves all orders with a total amount greater than $100 from the "orders" table:

SQL Copy code

```
SELECT order_id, total_amount
FROM orders
WHERE total_amount > 100;
```

In this example, the **WHERE** clause filters the data, ensuring that only rows where the "total_amount" is greater than $100 are included in the result set.

Combining Conditions

To retrieve orders with a total amount greater than $100 and placed in the year 2022, you'd use the following query:

SQL Copy code

```sql
SELECT order_id, total_amount, order_date
FROM orders
WHERE total_amount > 100 AND YEAR(order_date) = 2022
```

As you explore the depths of SQL's data manipulation capabilities, remember that the **SELECT** statement is your tool of choice for extracting the information you need. The ability to filter data using the **WHERE** clause is an essential skill that enables you to retrieve precise subsets of data and unleash the true potential of SQL.

Sorting and Grouping Results

In the realm of SQL, organizing and presenting data in a meaningful way is a skill that can provide invaluable insights. Two techniques that play a crucial role in this are sorting and grouping. Let's delve into how you can leverage these techniques to enhance the clarity and usefulness of your SQL queries.

Sorting Data with ORDER BY

Often, retrieving data in its raw form isn't sufficient. You might want to arrange the results in a specific order to make analysis easier.

The basic structure of an **ORDER BY** clause is as follows:

SQL Copy code

```
SELECT column1, column2, ...
FROM table_name
ORDER BY column1, column2, ...;
```

For example, to retrieve a list of employee names sorted alphabetically by their last names, you'd use the following query:

SQL Copy code

```
SELECT first_name, last_name
FROM employees
ORDER BY last_name;
```

By default, sorting is performed in ascending order. To sort in descending order, you can use the keyword **DESC**:

SQL Copy code

```sql
SELECT product_name, unit_price
FROM products
ORDER BY unit_price DESC;
```

Grouping Data with GROUP BY

Often, you'll want to aggregate data based on specific criteria. The **GROUP BY** clause allows you to group rows that share the same values in one or more columns. This is immensely useful for summarizing and analyzing data.

The basic structure of a **GROUP BY** clause is as follows:

SQL Copy code

```sql
SELECT column1, aggregate_function(column2)
FROM table_name
GROUP BY column1;
```

Consider a scenario where you want to find the total sales amount for each product category.

SQL Copy code

```
SELECT category_id, SUM(unit_price * quantity) AS total_sales
FROM order_details
GROUP BY category_id;
```

In this query, the **SUM** function aggregates the sales amount for each category, and the **GROUP BY** clause groups the results by the "category_id" column.

Combining **ORDER BY** and **GROUP BY** can provide even deeper insights. For instance, if you want to find the highest total sales for each product category, you'd use both clauses together:

SQL Copy code

```
SELECT category_id, SUM(unit_price * quantity) AS total_sales
FROM order_details
GROUP BY category_id
ORDER BY total_sales DESC;
```

By mastering the art of sorting and grouping data, you'll be equipped to not only retrieve information but also present it in a structured and insightful manner. These techniques are essential tools for any SQL practitioner seeking to derive actionable insights from their data.

Aggregation Functions for Data Analysis

When it comes to making sense of data, SQL offers a powerful arsenal of aggregation functions that allow you to perform calculations on groups of rows and derive meaningful insights. These functions aggregate data and provide you with summaries that aid in analysis. Let's explore some of the essential aggregation functions and their applications.

COUNT: Counting Records

The **COUNT** function tallies the number of records in a specified column. It's useful for understanding the size of a dataset or counting occurrences that meet specific criteria.

SQL Copy code

```sql
SELECT COUNT(*) AS total_customers
FROM customers;
```

SUM: Adding Values

The **SUM** function calculates the total sum of numeric values within a column. It's invaluable for calculating cumulative totals, such as the overall revenue generated from sales.

SQL Copy code

```sql
SELECT SUM(total_amount) AS total_revenue FROM orders;
```

AVG: Finding Averages

The **AVG** function calculates the average of numeric values within a column. It's ideal for assessing trends and understanding the typical value of a dataset.

```sql
language-sql

SELECT AVG(unit_price) AS average_price FROM products;
```

MIN and MAX: Finding Extremes

The **MIN** function returns the smallest value in a column, while the **MAX** function returns the largest. They're useful for identifying minimum and maximum values within a dataset.

```sql
language-sql

SELECT MIN(unit_price) AS lowest_price, MAX(unit_price) AS highest_price FROM products;
```

GROUP BY with Aggregation Functions

Aggregation functions are often used in conjunction with the **GROUP BY** clause to perform calculations on grouped data. For instance, to find the total sales amount for each customer:

```sql
language-sql

SELECT customer_id, SUM(total_amount) AS total_sales
FROM orders
GROUP BY customer_id;
```

HAVING: Filtering Grouped Data

The **HAVING** clause is used with grouped data to filter results based on aggregated values. For instance, to find customers who placed orders with a total amount greater than $1,000:

```sql
SELECT customer_id, SUM(total_amount) AS total_spent
FROM orders
GROUP BY customer_id
HAVING total_spent > 1000;
```

Aggregation functions are powerful tools for conducting data analysis within SQL. By utilizing these functions, you can uncover trends, patterns, and summaries that provide a deeper understanding of your datasets. Whether you're calculating averages, identifying extremes, or summarizing group-level data, these functions enhance your ability to glean valuable insights from your data.

Chapter 3: Joining and Combining Data

In the world of databases, data is often distributed across multiple tables. Joining and combining data from these tables is a fundamental skill that enables you to create comprehensive datasets for analysis. This chapter delves into the art of joining data through various types of joins—inner, outer, left, and right joins.

Inner Joins: Bridging Related Data

Inner joins are the foundation of combining data. They retrieve only the matching records between two tables based on a specified condition. This condition is usually a common column—often a primary key in one table and a foreign key in another.

The basic structure of an inner join is as follows:

```sql
language-sql

SELECT column1, column2, ...
FROM table1
INNER JOIN table2 ON table1.column = table2.column;
```

For example, imagine you have an "orders" table and a "customers" table. To retrieve a list of orders along with the corresponding customer names, you'd use an inner join:

```language-sql
SELECT order_id, order_date, customer_name
FROM orders
INNER JOIN customers ON orders.customer_id = customers.customer_id;
```

Outer Joins: Including Non-Matching Data

While inner joins focus on matching data, **outer joins** take a broader approach. They retrieve matching records as well as any non-matching records from one table.

```language-sql
SELECT column1, column2, ...
FROM table1
LEFT OUTER JOIN table2
ON table1.column = table2.column;
```

Right Outer Join

A **right outer join** is similar to a left outer join, but it retrieves all records from the right table and the matching records from the left table.

```sql
language-sql

SELECT column1, column2, ...
FROM table1
RIGHT OUTER JOIN table2
ON table1.column = table2.column;
```

Left and Right Joins in One Example

To illustrate both left and right joins, consider a scenario where you want to retrieve all customers and their associated orders, including customers who haven't placed any orders:

```sql
language-sql

SELECT customer_name, order_id
FROM customers
LEFT OUTER JOIN orders ON customers.customer_id = orders.customer_id;
```

```sql
language-sql

SELECT customer_name, order_id
FROM customers
RIGHT OUTER JOIN orders
ON customers.customer_id = orders.customer_id;
```

Full Outer Joins: Comprehensive Matching

A **full outer join** retrieves all records from both tables, matching where possible and filling in null values for non-matching records.

```sql
SELECT column1, column2, ...
FROM table1
FULL OUTER JOIN table2
ON table1.column = table2.column;
```

Understanding inner, outer, left, and right joins empowers you to bring together related data from various tables. This skill is pivotal for creating comprehensive datasets and extracting insights that would remain hidden in isolated tables. By mastering the art of data combination, you unlock a world of analytical possibilities within SQL.

Cross Joins and Self-Joins

Beyond the realm of inner and outer joins, SQL offers more specialized techniques for combining data: **cross joins** and **self-joins**. These techniques expand your capabilities in creating versatile datasets and exploring complex relationships within your data.

Cross Joins: Exploring All Combinations

This results in a combination of all possible pairs of rows from both tables. Cross joins are rarely used for large datasets, as they can produce a vast number of results.

The basic structure of a cross join is as follows:

SQL Copy code

```
SELECT column1, column2, ...
FROM table1
CROSS JOIN table2;
```

For instance, consider a situation where you want to generate all possible combinations of products and colors:

SQL Copy code

```
SELECT product_name, color_name
FROM products
CROSS JOIN colors;
```

Self-Joins: Unveiling Intra-Table Relationships

A **self-join** involves joining a table with itself. This technique is used to explore relationships within a single table, often when that table contains hierarchical or interconnected data. By giving the table aliases, you distinguish between the different instances of the same table.

For instance, imagine a "employees" table where each employee has a manager identified by their manager ID:

SQL Copy code

```
SELECT e.employee_name, m.employee_name AS manager_name
FROM employees e
INNER JOIN employees m ON e.manager_id = m.employee_id;
```

In this query, we're joining the "employees" table with itself to retrieve both the employee's name and the name of their manager.

Combining Techniques for Advanced Insights

While cross joins and self-joins might seem niche, they can be incredibly valuable in uncovering complex relationships within your data. Cross joins are particularly useful for scenarios like generating all possible combinations for analysis, while self-joins help reveal hierarchical or network-based patterns within a single table.

As you master these advanced joining techniques, you'll gain the ability to explore data from new angles and unearth insights that would be challenging to discover with simpler join types. These techniques elevate your SQL skills, enabling you to tackle intricate data scenarios with confidence.

Chapter 4: Advanced Query Optimization

Indexing and its Impact on Performance

As SQL practitioners, optimizing query performance is a constant pursuit. One of the most potent tools in your optimization arsenal is **indexing**. Indexes are akin to the index of a book—they provide a way to quickly locate specific information within a dataset. Understanding indexing and its impact on query performance is key to creating efficient and responsive databases.

The Role of Indexes

An index is a data structure that enhances data retrieval speed. Instead of scanning an entire table to find specific rows, SQL can utilize indexes to swiftly pinpoint the desired data. Indexes are created on one or more columns of a table and are crucial for optimizing queries that involve filtering, sorting, and joining data.

Types of Indexes

There are different types of indexes, each with its own use cases:

- **B-Tree Index**: The most common type, it's suitable for equality and range queries.

- **Bitmap Index**: Efficient for columns with a limited number of distinct values.

- **Hash Index**: Ideal for exact-match lookups.

- **Full-Text Index**: Designed for searching text within large strings.

Creating Indexes

Creating an index involves choosing the columns to index and then using the **CREATE INDEX** statement. While indexing can significantly boost query performance, it's important to strike a balance—too many indexes can lead to overhead during data modification operations.

SQL Copy code

```sql
CREATE INDEX idx_product_name ON products (product_name);
```

Impact on Performance

Indexes accelerate query execution, but they also have trade-offs. While reading data becomes faster, indexes require space and incur a slight overhead during data insertion, update, and deletion operations. It's essential to choose indexing strategies based on the type of queries frequently run on your data.

Choosing Columns to Index

Deciding which columns to index depends on the queries you commonly execute. Columns with low cardinality might not benefit from indexing as much as those with high cardinality.

Monitoring and Maintaining Indexes

As your database grows, it's crucial to monitor index usage and periodically assess their effectiveness. Unused or redundant indexes should be removed, and indexes that impact performance negatively might need adjustments.

Summary

Indexing is a powerful tool for enhancing query performance by minimizing the time spent searching through data. By strategically selecting columns to index and monitoring their impact, you can strike the right balance between responsiveness and efficiency in your SQL database. Mastery of indexing is a hallmark of SQL expertise, and it's a skill that can significantly impact the user experience of your applications.

Subqueries and their Practical Applications

In the realm of SQL, **subqueries** (also known as nested queries or inner queries) are a versatile tool for performing complex operations by embedding one query within another. Subqueries allow you to break down complex problems into manageable parts and solve them step by step. Let's explore the concept of subqueries and how they find practical applications in various scenarios.

Understanding Subqueries

At its core, a subquery is a query that is nested within another query. The result of the inner query is used as a value or condition in the outer query. Subqueries can be placed in various parts of a SQL statement, such as within the **SELECT**, **FROM**, or **WHERE** clauses.

Practical Applications of Subqueries

1. **Filtering Data with Subqueries**: Subqueries within the **WHERE** clause help filter results based on conditions that involve data from multiple tables. For instance, you can retrieve a list of customers who have placed orders above the average order amount:

SQL Copy code

```
SELECT customer_name
FROM customers
WHERE customer_id IN (
    SELECT customer_id
    FROM orders
    WHERE order_amount > (
        SELECT AVG(order_amount)
        FROM orders
    )
);
```

2. **Calculations and Aggregations**: Subqueries can be used to perform calculations or aggregations on a subset of data. For example, you can retrieve products whose price is higher than the average price:

SQL Copy code

```
SELECT product_name
FROM products
WHERE unit_price > (SELECT AVG(unit_price) FROM products);
```

3. **Subqueries in the SELECT Clause**: Subqueries can be used within the **SELECT** clause to retrieve specific values for each row. For instance, you can

retrieve the number of orders placed by each customer:

SQL Copy code

```sql
SELECT customer_name
FROM customers c
WHERE (
    SELECT AVG(order_amount)
    FROM orders
    WHERE orders.customer_id = c.customer_id
) < ALL (
    SELECT order_amount
    FROM orders
    WHERE orders.customer_id = c.customer_id
);
```

4. **Correlated Subqueries**: Correlated subqueries reference values from the outer query, allowing for dynamic comparisons. For example, you can find customers who have placed orders exceeding their average order amount:

SQL Copy code

```
SELECT customer_name
FROM customers c
WHERE (SELECT AVG(order_amount) FROM orders WHERE orders.customer_id = c.customer_id)
< ALL (SELECT order_amount FROM orders WHERE orders.customer_id = c.customer_id);
```

Subqueries are a powerful tool that enables you to solve complex problems efficiently. By breaking down tasks into smaller components, subqueries enhance the readability and maintainability of your SQL code. As you master subqueries, you'll find creative ways to manipulate and analyze data across various scenarios.

Common Table Expressions (CTEs) for Enhanced Readability

In the pursuit of writing clear and maintainable SQL queries, **Common Table Expressions** (CTEs) emerge as a powerful tool. CTEs provide a way to break down complex queries into manageable and easily understandable sections. By creating temporary result sets that you can reference multiple times within a larger query, CTEs enhance readability, facilitate debugging, and streamline your SQL code.

Basic Structure of a CTE

A CTE is defined using the **WITH** keyword, followed by the CTE name and its definition. It resembles the structure of a subquery but offers more flexibility and clarity.

SQL Copy code

```
WITH cte_name (column1, column2, ...)
AS
(
    SELECT ...
    FROM ...
    WHERE ...
)
```

Benefits of Using CTEs

1. **Enhanced Readability**: By separating complex logic into modular sections, CTEs make your query easier to understand and maintain. Each CTE provides a descriptive name for a specific subset of data.

2. **Avoiding Repetition**: CTEs allow you to define a query once and reference it multiple times within the same query. This reduces redundancy and ensures consistency in your code.

3. **Simplified Debugging**: Isolating each CTE lets you focus on troubleshooting specific sections of your query, making it simpler to identify and rectify errors.

Practical Applications of CTEs

1. **Recursive Queries**: CTEs are ideal for recursive queries, where a query references itself multiple times. This is particularly useful for hierarchical data like organizational charts or threaded discussions.

2. **Aggregations and Transformations**: CTEs can simplify complex aggregations or transformations by breaking them down into separate steps. This enhances clarity and readability.

3. **Multiple Calculations**: When you need to perform multiple calculations on the same subset of data, CTEs allow you to create intermediary result sets that can be easily reused.

Example of Using CTEs

Imagine a scenario where you want to find customers who have placed orders above the average order amount. Using a CTE, you can achieve this in a well-organized manner:

SQL Copy code

```sql
WITH AverageOrders AS (
    SELECT AVG(order_amount) AS avg_order_amount
    FROM orders
)
SELECT customer_name
FROM customers
JOIN AverageOrders ON orders.order_amount > AverageOrders.avg_order_amount;
```

This result is then joined with the "customers" table to retrieve the desired information.

Mastering CTEs for Clearer Queries

By embracing Common Table Expressions, you elevate your SQL coding practices. CTEs provide an elegant solution for tackling complex queries while maintaining readability and structure. As you become proficient with CTEs, you'll find yourself crafting queries that are not only powerful but also comprehensible to both you and your colleagues.

Chapter 5: Working with Complex Data Types

Handling Dates, Times, and Time Zones

In the realm of data manipulation, dealing with date and time information requires a specialized skill set. SQL offers a range of functions and techniques to effectively manage these complex data types, ensuring accuracy, consistency, and ease of use. This chapter explores the intricacies of handling dates, times, and time zones within SQL.

Understanding Date and Time Data Types

SQL supports various data types for storing date and time information, including **DATE**, **TIME**, **DATETIME**, and **TIMESTAMP**. These data types allow you to represent specific moments in time, durations, or intervals.

Working with Dates and Times

SQL provides a multitude of functions to manipulate date and time data:

- **EXTRACT**: Extracts specific components (year, month, day, etc.) from a date or time.

- **DATE_ADD** and **DATE_SUB**: Add or subtract intervals from dates.

- **DATE_DIFF**: Calculate the difference between two dates in terms of a specific unit (days, months, etc.).

- **DATE_FORMAT**: Converts date and time values into specific string formats.

Time Zones and Timestamps

When dealing with data across different geographical locations, accounting for time zones is crucial. The **TIMESTAMP WITH TIME ZONE** data type helps manage time zone information, allowing you to store and retrieve timestamps in a way that respects time zone differences.

Dealing with Daylight Saving Time

Daylight Saving Time (DST) shifts complicate time-related calculations. SQL functions like **CONVERT_TZ** enable you to convert timestamps across time zones, considering DST changes.

Practical Applications

1. **Calculating Age**: By subtracting birth dates from the current date, you can calculate precise ages of individuals.

2. **Date Ranges**: SQL's date and time functions are useful for filtering and aggregating data within specific date ranges.

3. **Temporal Data Analysis**: Analyzing trends over time, tracking historical changes, and forecasting require efficient date and time manipulation.

4. **Event Scheduling**: Systems that manage events, appointments, or deadlines rely heavily on accurate date and time calculations.

Example: Handling Time Zones

Suppose you're managing a global event registration system. You want to list all events and their start times, considering the attendees' local time zones:

SQL Copy code

```sql
SELECT event_name, CONVERT_TZ(event_start_time, 'UTC', user_time_zone) AS local_start_time
FROM events
JOIN users ON events.organizer_id = users.user_id;
```

In this example, the **CONVERT_TZ** function transforms event start times from UTC to each user's specified time zone.

Mastering Time Manipulation

Effectively managing dates, times, and time zones within SQL requires a deep understanding of the available functions and data types. This knowledge empowers you to accurately analyze temporal data, accommodate global audiences, and optimize various time-related operations. As you navigate this complex landscape, your expertise in handling time-related data will set you apart as a skilled SQL practitioner.

Dealing with Strings and Textual Data

In the world of SQL, the handling of strings and textual data is a fundamental skill that enables you to manipulate and analyze textual information effectively. Whether you're searching for specific patterns, transforming data, or combining strings, SQL provides a rich set of functions to cater to various string-related tasks. This chapter explores techniques to deal with strings and textual data within SQL.

Manipulating Textual Data

SQL offers an array of functions to manipulate strings, including:

- **UPPER** and **LOWER**: Converts text to uppercase or lowercase.

- **SUBSTRING**: Extracts a portion of a string based on starting and ending positions.

- **TRIM**: Removes specified characters from the beginning and/or end of a string.

Pattern Matching with LIKE and Regular Expressions

The **LIKE** operator allows for simple pattern matching using wildcards: **%** (matches any sequence of characters) and _ (matches a single character). For more advanced pattern matching, SQL supports regular expressions using functions like **REGEXP**.

Concatenating and Formatting Strings

String concatenation is a common operation in SQL. You can combine text strings with data retrieved from columns using the **CONCAT** function or the || operator. Additionally, the **FORMAT** function allows for sophisticated string formatting, which is particularly useful for displaying dates, times, and numerical values.

Practical Applications

1. **Data Cleansing and Transformation**: String functions play a crucial role in cleaning and transforming raw data, like removing unnecessary characters or formatting data consistently.

2. **Generating Custom Outputs**: You can generate customized outputs for reports, emails, or user interfaces by skillfully combining and formatting strings.

3. **Text Search and Analysis**: SQL's string manipulation capabilities are invaluable when performing text-based searches, analyzing sentiment, or categorizing textual data.

Example: Extracting Initials

Imagine you have a database of employees' first names and want to retrieve their initials:

SQL Copy code

```sql
SELECT first_name, CONCAT(LEFT(first_name, 1), '.') AS initials FROM employees;
```

In this example, the **LEFT** function extracts the first letter of each employee's first name, and then the **CONCAT** function combines it with a period to form the initials.

Harnessing the Power of Strings

The ability to effectively handle strings and textual data expands your toolkit as a SQL practitioner. Whether you're crafting elegant reports, conducting text-based analyses, or transforming data, mastering string manipulation functions allows you to wield SQL's capabilities to their fullest extent. As you delve into the intricacies of string manipulation, you empower yourself to craft precise and impactful queries.

Storing and Retrieving Binary Data

In addition to handling textual and numerical data, SQL is capable of managing binary data—information stored in the form of sequences of bytes. Binary data includes files such as images, audio, video, and other non-textual formats. SQL provides mechanisms to store, retrieve, and manipulate binary data efficiently.

Binary Data Types

SQL offers various binary data types to accommodate different types of binary information:

- **BLOB (Binary Large Object)**: Suitable for storing large amounts of binary data, such as images, videos, or documents.

- **BINARY**: Used for fixed-length binary data.

- **VARBINARY**: Used for variable-length binary data.

Storing Binary Data

When inserting binary data, you need to convert it into a suitable format. Most programming languages and frameworks provide methods to convert binary data into a format that can be inserted into a BLOB column.

SQL Copy code

```
INSERT INTO media (media_content) VALUES (CONVERT(binary_data, BINARY));
```

Retrieving Binary Data

Retrieving binary data involves converting it back to its original format using the appropriate programming language or tool. In SQL, you can retrieve binary data using the **SELECT** statement:

SQL Copy code

```
SELECT media_content FROM media WHERE media_id = 123;
```

Practical Applications

1. **Storing Media Assets**: BLOB columns are commonly used to store images, videos, audio files, and other media assets associated with records in a database.

2. **Document Management**: Binary data types are useful for storing documents, spreadsheets, presentations, or any other type of file within a database.

3. **Data Serialization**: Storing serialized objects or data structures for application-specific use cases.

Example: Storing Images

Imagine you have an online store database and you want to associate product images with each product. You can use a BLOB column to store the image data:

SQL Copy code

```
CREATE TABLE products (
    product_id INT PRIMARY KEY,
    product_name VARCHAR(255),
    product_image BLOB
);

INSERT INTO products (product_id, product_name, product_image)
VALUES (1, 'Smartphone', CONVERT(binary_image_data, BINARY));
```

In this example, the column "product_image" is a BLOB column where the binary image data is stored.

Harnessing the Flexibility of Binary Data

By embracing binary data storage in SQL, you broaden the capabilities of your database system. From multimedia assets to custom data serialization, handling binary data extends the usefulness of SQL in various applications. As you navigate the world of binary data, you gain the ability to store and retrieve a wide range of non-textual information efficiently and effectively.

Chapter 6: Managing Databases and Tables

Creating, Modifying, and Deleting Databases

The foundation of any SQL-based application lies in its databases and tables. Effectively managing these components is essential for maintaining data integrity, performance, and organizational efficiency. This chapter delves into the intricacies of creating, modifying, and deleting databases—crucial tasks that lay the groundwork for a robust database environment.

Creating Databases

Creating a database is the first step in organizing your data. SQL provides the **CREATE DATABASE** statement to establish a new database. You can specify various parameters, such as the character set and collation, to ensure data consistency across different languages and regions.

SQL Copy code

```sql
CREATE DATABASE my_database CHARACTER SET utf8mb4 COLLATE utf8mb4_unicode_ci;
```

Modifying Databases

Database modification involves changing its attributes, such as its character set or collation. However, SQL's capabilities for altering databases are limited compared to altering tables. Most of the time, you'll need to create a new database with the desired attributes and migrate data from the old database.

Deleting Databases

When a database is no longer needed, SQL provides the **DROP DATABASE** statement to remove it. Keep in mind that dropping a database is a significant action that irreversibly deletes all the data and tables within it.

SQL Copy code

```sql
DROP DATABASE my_database;
```

Backup and Restore

Maintaining database backups is vital to ensure data integrity and recovery in case of unexpected events. Many database management systems offer tools to create and manage backups, allowing you to restore your database to a previous state.

Practical Applications

1. **Development and Testing**: Creating separate databases for development, testing, and production environments helps maintain a clean separation of data.

2. **Data Partitioning**: When data grows too large, partitioning—splitting tables across multiple databases—can improve performance and manageability.

3. **Database Migration**: Modifying databases or migrating data between databases is essential during application upgrades or data center shifts.

Example: Creating a Database

Suppose you're developing a content management system and need a database to store user-generated content:

SQL Copy code

```
CREATE DATABASE cms_db CHARACTER SET utf8mb4 COLLATE utf8mb4_unicode_ci;
```

In this example, the **CREATE DATABASE** statement establishes the "cms_db" database with the specified character set and collation.

Mastering Database Management

Efficiently creating, modifying, and deleting databases are foundational skills in database management. The careful execution of these tasks ensures data integrity, optimizes performance, and streamlines database administration. As you navigate the world of database management, you'll develop the expertise to establish and maintain a robust database environment that supports your application's needs.

let's talk about some key principles and best practices when it comes to designing tables in a database. Think of tables as the building blocks of your database, so getting their design right is crucial for the overall efficiency and organization of your data.

1. **Keep it Simple and Organized**: Each table should have a clear purpose. Avoid cramming unrelated data into one table. If you find yourself adding too many columns, it might be a sign that your table is trying to do too much.

2. **Follow Normalization Rules**: Normalization helps prevent data redundancy and ensures data integrity. Break your data into smaller logical pieces

and create separate tables for them. This reduces data duplication and makes updates easier.

3. **Choose Meaningful Names**: Naming conventions matter. Use descriptive names that make it easy to understand what each table represents. For instance, instead of "tbl_data," go for something like "customers" or "orders."

4. **Use Primary Keys**: Each table should have a primary key, a unique identifier for each row. This helps ensure data uniqueness and efficient querying.

5. **Data Types Matter**: Choose appropriate data types for columns. Don't use large data types for small amounts of data, as it wastes space. Also, consider future scalability; if a smallint might not be sufficient in the long run, go for an int.

6. **Indexes for Performance**: Indexes speed up data retrieval. Identify columns frequently used in search conditions or joins and create indexes on them. But be cautious; too many indexes can slow down data modification operations.

7. **Mind Relationships**: If your data involves relationships (like a customer placing orders), establish foreign key relationships between tables. This helps maintain data integrity and supports querying across related data.

8. **Avoid Over-Normalization**: While normalization is good, overdoing it can complicate queries. Finding the right balance between normalization and query efficiency is key.

9. **Consider Growth and Scalability**: Your table design should accommodate future growth. Design your tables in a way that allows you to add new data without drastically altering the structure.

10. **Document Your Design**: Keep documentation about your table structure, relationships, and any specific considerations. This helps other team members understand the database's architecture.

11. **Testing is Crucial**: Before deploying your database, test your table design with sample data and various types of queries. This ensures that your design supports the real-world scenarios your application will face.

12. **Regular Maintenance**: Over time, revisit your table design. If the application's requirements change, your database might need adjustments to stay efficient.

Remember, table design isn't set in stone. It's a dynamic process that evolves with your application and its requirements. A well-designed database can significantly enhance the performance, maintainability, and scalability of your application.

Constraints and Data Integrity

When it comes to maintaining the quality and consistency of your data, **constraints** play a critical role. Constraints are rules applied to the columns of a table, ensuring that the data entered meets specific criteria. They safeguard your data integrity and help prevent erroneous or inconsistent data from polluting your database.

Types of Constraints

1. **Primary Key Constraint**: Ensures that each row in a table has a unique identifier. It prevents duplicate entries and serves as the basis for establishing relationships between tables.

2. **Foreign Key Constraint**: Creates a link between two tables, enforcing referential integrity. It ensures that values in one table's column match values in another table's primary key column.

3. **Unique Constraint**: Guarantees that values in a column are unique across the table. Unlike primary keys, unique constraints allow null values, enabling columns to have unique values or null.

4. **Check Constraint**: Allows you to define specific conditions that data must meet. For instance, you can use check constraints to ensure that ages are positive numbers.

Importance of Constraints

1. **Data Accuracy**: Constraints prevent data that doesn't adhere to your defined rules from being entered.

2. **Referential Integrity**: Foreign key constraints maintain the relationship between tables, preventing orphaned records and maintaining data coherence.

3. **Consistency**: Constraints ensure uniform data across the database, eliminating discrepancies that could arise from manual data entry errors.

Practical Applications

1. **Preventing Inconsistent Data**: A unique constraint on email addresses prevents users from registering with the same email multiple times.

2. **Maintaining Relationships**: Foreign key constraints ensure that an order is associated with an existing customer and that a product is associated with a valid category.

3. **Data Validation**: Check constraints can ensure that dates are within a certain range or that certain fields are not left empty.

Example: Using Constraints

Suppose you're designing a database for an online library. You want to ensure that each book in your system has a unique ISBN and that all borrowed books are associated with valid users:

SQL Copy code

```sql
CREATE TABLE books (
  book_id INT PRIMARY KEY,
  title VARCHAR(255),
  isbn VARCHAR(13) UNIQUE,
  author VARCHAR(255)
);

CREATE TABLE borrowings (
  borrowing_id INT PRIMARY KEY,
  book_id INT,
  user_id INT,
  borrow_date DATE,
  return_date DATE,
  FOREIGN KEY (book_id) REFERENCES books(book_id),
  FOREIGN KEY (user_id) REFERENCES users(user_id)
);
```

In this example, the **UNIQUE** constraint on the "isbn" column ensures that no two books have the same ISBN. The **FOREIGN KEY** constraints on the "book_id" and "user_id" columns in the "borrowings" table maintain the relationships with the "books" and "users" tables, respectively.

Safeguarding Your Data with Constraints

Constraints are your database's guardians, ensuring that only valid, consistent, and reliable data makes its way into your tables. By enforcing rules and relationships, constraints are integral to maintaining the integrity of your data and the functionality of your applications.

Chapter 7: Stored Procedures and Functions

Creating and Executing Stored Procedures

Stored procedures and functions are powerful tools that encapsulate a set of SQL statements into a reusable unit. They offer a way to organize your code, enhance security, and improve performance by reducing the need for repetitive SQL execution. In this chapter, we'll delve into the creation and execution of stored procedures and functions.

Stored Procedures

It's particularly useful for complex database operations or tasks that need to be performed repeatedly.

Creating a stored procedure involves defining its name, parameters, and the SQL statements it should execute:

SQL Copy code

```
CREATE PROCEDURE sp_GetCustomerOrders (IN customer_id INT)
BEGIN
    SELECT * FROM orders WHERE customer_id = customer_id;
END;
```

You can then execute the stored procedure by calling it with appropriate parameters:

SQL Copy code

```
CALL sp_GetCustomerOrders(123);
```

Functions

Functions are similar to stored procedures but are designed to return a single value. They are commonly used in SQL expressions to perform calculations or retrieve specific data.

Creating a function involves specifying its name, parameters, and the SQL statement that returns the desired value:

SQL Copy code

```
CREATE FUNCTION fn_CalculateDiscount (IN order_total DECIMAL(10,2))
RETURNS DECIMAL(10,2)
BEGIN
    DECLARE discount DECIMAL(10,2);
    IF order_total > 100 THEN
        SET discount = order_total * 0.1;
    ELSE
        SET discount = 0;
    END IF;
    RETURN discount;
END;
```

You can use the function in queries like this:

SQL Copy code

SELECT order_id, order_total, fn_CalculateDiscount(order_total) AS discount FROM orders;

Practical Applications

1. **Code Reusability**: Stored procedures and functions reduce code duplication by encapsulating logic into a single unit that can be reused across multiple parts of your application.

2. **Performance Optimization**: Precompiled stored procedures can improve performance by reducing the overhead of sending multiple SQL statements to the database server.

3. **Security**: You can grant permissions to execute stored procedures without giving users direct access to underlying tables, enhancing data security.

Example: Order Total Calculation

Imagine you need to calculate the total cost of an order including tax and shipping for a specific customer. You can create a stored procedure to handle this complex calculation:

SQL Copy code

```sql
CREATE PROCEDURE sp_CalculateOrderTotal (IN order_id INT)
BEGIN
    DECLARE total DECIMAL(10,2);

    SELECT (order_amount + (order_amount * tax_rate) + shipping_cost) INTO total
    FROM orders
    WHERE order_id = order_id;

    SELECT total;
END;
```

You can then call this stored procedure to get the calculated order total:

SQL Copy code

```sql
CALL sp_CalculateOrderTotal(456);
```

Empowering Code Organization

Stored procedures and functions provide a structured way to encapsulate and reuse your SQL code. By centralizing complex operations and logic, you enhance code readability, maintainability, and performance. As you integrate these tools into your SQL toolkit, you'll streamline your database interactions and empower your applications with more efficient and organized data manipulation.

User-Defined Functions for Custom Operations

User-Defined Functions (UDFs) extend the capabilities of your database by enabling you to define custom operations that can be used within SQL queries. UDFs offer a way to encapsulate complex calculations, transformations, or business logic, making your queries more expressive and efficient. Let's explore how to create and use UDFs to enhance your SQL experience.

Creating User-Defined Functions

To create a UDF, you define its name, parameters, return type, and the logic it should execute. UDFs can be scalar functions (returning a single value) or table-valued functions (returning a table-like result set).

Here's an example of creating a scalar UDF that calculates the total price of an order with tax and discount:

SQL Copy code

```
CREATE FUNCTION fn_CalculateTotalPrice (order_amount DECIMAL(10,2), tax_rate DECIMAL(5,2), discount DECIMAL(5,2))
RETURNS DECIMAL(10,2)
BEGIN
    DECLARE total_price DECIMAL(10,2);
    SET total_price = order_amount + (order_amount * tax_rate) - (order_amount * discount);
    RETURN total_price;
END;
```

Using User-Defined Functions

Once you've created a UDF, you can seamlessly integrate it into your queries, treating it like any built-in SQL function. UDFs can be used in SELECT statements, WHERE clauses, and even in other functions.

Here's an example of using the previously defined UDF to retrieve orders with their calculated total prices:

SQL Copy code

```
SELECT order_id, order_amount, tax_rate, discount,
fn_CalculateTotalPrice(order_amount, tax_rate, discount) AS total_price FROM orders;
```

Advantages of User-Defined Functions

1. **Code Reusability**: UDFs allow you to reuse custom logic across multiple queries, promoting code efficiency and consistency.

2. **Modular Design**: By encapsulating complex logic in UDFs, you improve code organization and readability, making your queries more manageable.

3. **Abstraction**: UDFs abstract complex calculations into a single function call, making your queries more concise and human-readable.

Example: Text Case Conversion

Suppose you want to create a UDF that converts text to title case. You can define a scalar UDF like this:

SQL Copy code

```
CREATE FUNCTION fn_TitleCase (input_text VARCHAR(255)) RETURNS VARCHAR(255)
BEGIN
    DECLARE output_text VARCHAR(255);
    SET output_text = LOWER(input_text);
    SET output_text = CONCAT(UPPER(SUBSTRING(output_text, 1, 1)), SUBSTRING(output_text, 2));
    RETURN output_text;
END;
```

You can use this UDF to convert product names to title case:

SQL Copy code

```
SELECT product_id, product_name, fn_TitleCase(product_name) AS formatted_name FROM products;
```

Custom Functions, Powerful Queries

User-Defined Functions bring a new dimension to your SQL capabilities, allowing you to incorporate custom logic seamlessly into your queries. Whether you're performing intricate calculations, data transformations, or specialized text operations, UDFs empower you to create more expressive and efficient queries tailored to your specific needs.

Benefits of Using Procedural SQL

Procedural SQL introduces a layer of programming logic into your database interactions, offering several benefits that enhance your ability to manage, manipulate, and retrieve data. Let's explore the advantages of incorporating procedural SQL into your database development practices.

1. Logic Centralization

Procedural SQL, through features like stored procedures and functions, allows you to centralize complex logic within the database. This means that business rules, calculations, and data transformations are encapsulated in one place, promoting maintainability and reducing redundancy.

2. Reusability and Code Efficiency

Stored procedures and functions are reusable blocks of code that can be called from various parts of your application. This reusability not only saves development time but also ensures consistent implementation of logic across different queries and processes.

3. Security and Access Control

By using stored procedures, you can restrict direct access to tables and instead grant access only to specific procedures. This enhances security by preventing unauthorized users from manipulating data directly while still allowing them to perform permitted actions through the procedures.

4. Performance Optimization

Precompiled stored procedures can improve query performance by reducing the overhead of sending multiple SQL statements to the database server. Additionally, procedural SQL allows for more efficient data manipulation within the database, potentially reducing data transfer between the application and the database.

5. Data Integrity

With constraints and triggers, you can enforce data integrity rules directly within the database. This helps prevent inconsistent or erroneous data from being entered, maintaining the quality and reliability of your data.

6. Error Handling and Consistency

Procedural SQL enables you to implement robust error handling mechanisms. You can define how the database should respond to different types of errors, ensuring that your application gracefully handles unexpected situations.

7. Performance of Batch Operations

For tasks involving multiple rows or complex data transformations, procedural SQL can be significantly more efficient than retrieving data to the application, processing it, and sending it back to the database.

8. Reduced Network Traffic

When complex processing occurs within the database, there's less need to transfer large datasets back and forth between the application and the database, reducing network traffic and latency.

9. Integration with Application Logic

Procedural SQL can integrate seamlessly with your application's logic. You can leverage the power of the database alongside your application's programming language to create comprehensive solutions.

10. Simplified Client-Side Code

By offloading complex logic to the database, you can simplify your client-side application code. This leads to cleaner and more maintainable code in your application layer.

Enriching Data Management

Procedural SQL extends the capabilities of your database system beyond data storage and retrieval. It empowers you to manage, manipulate, and secure your data effectively while reducing the workload on your application. By tapping into the benefits of procedural SQL, you elevate your database interactions, streamline your development process, and create a more efficient and robust application environment.

Chapter 8: Advanced Data Analysis with Window Functions

Understanding Window Functions and Their Usage

Window functions are a powerful tool in SQL that allow you to perform calculations across a set of rows related to the current row. Unlike traditional aggregate functions, window functions maintain individual row-level details while providing insights into trends, rankings, and aggregations within specific windows of data. In this chapter, we explore the concepts and applications of window functions.

Ranking, Row Numbering, and Percentile Calculations

Window functions enable you to assign rankings, row numbers, and percentiles to rows based on specified criteria. This facilitates the identification of top performers, outliers, and distribution patterns within your data.

SQL Copy code

```sql
SELECT product_name, order_date, order_amount,
RANK() OVER (PARTITION BY product_name ORDER BY order_amount DESC) AS rank,
PERCENTILE_CONT(0.75) WITHIN GROUP (ORDER BY order_amount) OVER () AS p75
FROM sales;
```

In this example, the **RANK** function assigns a ranking to each product's orders based on order amount. The **PERCENTILE_CONT** function calculates the 75th percentile of all order amounts across the dataset.

Moving Averages and Rolling Aggregations

Window functions enable the calculation of moving averages and rolling aggregations, revealing trends and patterns over time. This is particularly useful for financial analysis, time series data, and performance tracking.

SQL Copy code

```sql
SELECT date, revenue, AVG(revenue) OVER
(ORDER BY date ROWS BETWEEN 3 PRECEDING AND 1 FOLLOWING) AS moving_avg FROM daily_revenue;
```

In this example, the **AVG** function calculates a moving average of revenue over a window of the three preceding rows and the current row.

Practical Applications

1. **Time Series Analysis**: Window functions help analyze trends, seasonality, and anomalies in time

series data by calculating aggregates over specified time windows.

2. **Segmentation and Ranking**: Identify top customers, best-selling products, or underperforming regions by ranking and segmenting data using window functions.

3. **Performance Metrics**: Calculate rolling averages or percentages to monitor key performance indicators (KPIs) and make informed decisions.

Example: Analyzing Sales Trends

Imagine you're analyzing sales data and want to understand the sales growth compared to the previous month. You can use a window function to calculate the percentage change.

Unveiling Insights with Window Functions

Window functions transform your SQL queries from simple data retrieval to advanced analytical tools. By providing context-aware calculations and insights, window functions offer a deeper understanding of your data's dynamics and patterns. As you master window functions, you unlock the potential to uncover hidden trends and make data-driven decisions with precision.

Consider the scenario of a retail business analyzing customer purchase behavior. Using window functions, you can effortlessly compute metrics like rolling averages of customer spending over specific time periods, identify customer segments with the highest growth rates, and even monitor the impact of promotional campaigns on different customer cohorts.

Furthermore, window functions empower you to tackle complex calculations directly within your SQL queries. This streamlines your data analysis workflow and reduces the need to export data to external tools for further processing. With the ability to perform calculations across ordered rows, partition data for targeted analysis, and discern changes in trends over time, you're equipped to explore your data on a whole new level.

As you delve into the intricacies of window functions, remember that their true power emerges when combined with other SQL features like joins, subqueries, and aggregations. The synergy of these tools allows you to construct intricate data narratives, offering insights that guide your strategies and steer your business decisions.

In the ever-evolving landscape of data analysis, window functions stand as a cornerstone of advanced querying. By embracing this powerful technique, you empower yourself to transform data into knowledge, unravel intricate patterns, and uncover the stories your data yearns to tell. As a data-driven explorer armed with window functions, you're poised to navigate the complexities of your data universe with confidence and precision.

Chapter 9: Securing Your SQL Environment

In today's data-driven world, security is paramount. Protecting your SQL environment is not just about safeguarding data; it's about maintaining the trust of customers, partners, and stakeholders. This chapter delves into the strategies and techniques you can employ to secure your SQL environment effectively.

Role-Based Access Control

Role-Based Access Control (RBAC) is a fundamental principle in database security. It involves assigning specific roles to users or groups and granting them access only to the resources they need for their tasks. This practice minimizes the risk of unauthorized access and limits potential damage.

Defining Roles and Permissions: Create roles based on job responsibilities, such as "Admin," "User," or "Manager." Assign appropriate permissions to each role, restricting access to sensitive data and operations.

Implementing Principle of Least Privilege: Follow the principle of least privilege, granting users only the permissions required to perform their tasks. Avoid granting excessive access rights, reducing the potential impact of a security breach.

Regular Review and Audit: Periodically review roles and permissions to ensure they align with current business needs. Conduct audits to identify any unauthorized or obsolete access.

Example: In a healthcare database, roles could include "Doctors," "Nurses," and "Administrators." Doctors might have access to medical records, while nurses might only access patient vital signs.

Encrypting Data and Protecting Sensitive Information

Data Encryption: Encrypting sensitive data ensures that even if unauthorized access occurs, the data remains unreadable. Use techniques like **Transparent Data Encryption (TDE)** to encrypt data at the storage level.

Field-Level Encryption: Sensitive fields like social security numbers or credit card details can be individually encrypted. This adds an extra layer of protection to high-value data.

Data Masking: Mask sensitive data for non-privileged users. Instead of showing the actual data, display a masked version to protect user privacy.

Key Management: Proper key management is crucial to maintaining the security of encrypted data. Safeguard encryption keys and ensure they are regularly rotated.

Example: In a financial database, credit card numbers could be encrypted, and only authorized users with decryption keys can access the actual values.

Preventing SQL Injection Attacks

SQL Injection Attacks: One of the most common security vulnerabilities, SQL injection occurs when attackers manipulate user input to execute malicious SQL queries. It can lead to data leakage, unauthorized access, and even complete database compromise.

Parameterized Queries: Use parameterized queries or prepared statements to separate user input from SQL queries. This prevents attackers from injecting malicious code.

Input Validation: Validate user input to ensure it adheres to expected formats and values. Reject input that contains unexpected characters or patterns.

Escaping User Input: If dynamic queries are necessary, escape user input to neutralize malicious characters that could lead to injection attacks.

Stored Procedures: Using stored procedures can mitigate the risk of injection attacks, as they provide a layer of abstraction between user input and the SQL statements executed.

Example: Imagine a login page. Instead of directly inserting user input into an SQL query, use parameterized queries to ensure the input is treated as data, not executable code.

Practical Implementation and Beyond

Regular Updates: Keep your database software, patches, and security protocols up to date to address known vulnerabilities.

Network Security: Secure network connections using encryption, firewalls, and proper configuration.

Auditing and Monitoring: Implement auditing mechanisms to track user activities and identify suspicious behavior. Monitor logs for any signs of unauthorized access.

User Training: Train users on security best practices. Raise awareness about phishing, social engineering, and password hygiene.

Collaboration with Security Experts: Collaborate with cybersecurity professionals to assess vulnerabilities, perform penetration testing, and implement best practices.

Fortifying Your SQL Environment

Securing your SQL environment requires a proactive and comprehensive approach. Role-based access control, encryption, and protection against SQL injection attacks are foundational steps in safeguarding your data and maintaining the trust of your stakeholders. By integrating these practices into your database management strategy and staying vigilant in the face of evolving threats, you lay a robust foundation for a secure SQL environment that underpins your organization's success.

Chapter 10: Working with External Data Sources

As a computer engineer navigating the intricate landscape of data integration, mastering the art of working with external data sources becomes paramount. In this chapter, we delve into the nuances of seamlessly importing, exporting, and integrating data from diverse origins, bridging the gap between your SQL environment and the vast digital universe beyond.

Importing and Exporting Data

Data flow is the lifeblood of digital ecosystems. Efficiently **importing and exporting data** between your SQL databases and external sources is the cornerstone of modern data engineering.

Data Formats: Navigate through CSVs, JSON, XML, and other formats with finesse. Understand data structures to facilitate smooth data translation.

Data Transformation: Leverage tools for transforming data during import/export, ensuring seamless integration despite differences in structure.

Automated Workflows: Implement automated pipelines to synchronize data, reducing manual effort and increasing data consistency.

Example: Utilize SQL's native **COPY** command to efficiently load large datasets from CSV files, ensuring rapid data ingestion.

Integrating SQL with NoSQL and Web Services

In an era of diverse data paradigms, the synergy between SQL and NoSQL databases is invaluable. **Integrating SQL with NoSQL** involves bridging structured and unstructured data realms.

Polyglot Persistence: Understand the strengths of SQL and NoSQL databases, choosing the right tool for the job based on data requirements.

Data Mapping: Develop strategies for mapping data between SQL and NoSQL structures, preserving data integrity.

Hybrid Models: Explore hybrid models where SQL and NoSQL databases coexist, allowing you to leverage each database's strengths.

Example: Employ a relational database for structured user data while leveraging a NoSQL database for storing user-generated content.

Connecting to APIs and External APIs

In the era of interconnected applications, mastering the art of connecting to **APIs** and external APIs is a hallmark of modern data engineering.

RESTful APIs: Grasp the principles of RESTful architecture, enabling seamless interaction with external web services.

OAuth and API Keys: Understand authentication mechanisms like OAuth and API keys to securely access external APIs.

Data Enrichment: Harness the power of external APIs to enrich your data with real-time information, enhancing your application's value.

Error Handling and Rate Limiting: Implement error handling strategies and respect rate limits to ensure smooth API interactions.

Example: Connect to a weather API to enrich your customer database with real-time weather conditions based on user location.

Pushing Boundaries in Data Integration

As a computer engineer, your prowess extends beyond the confines of structured databases. Embrace the role of a digital architect, seamlessly integrating SQL with diverse data sources to form a cohesive data ecosystem.

Data Governance: Develop data governance strategies to maintain data quality and integrity across heterogeneous sources.

Streaming Data: Venture into the realm of real-time data streaming, integrating SQL databases with streams of live data.

Machine Learning Integration: Push the boundaries further by integrating SQL with machine learning models, enabling predictive insights.

Cybersecurity and Privacy: As you connect your SQL environment with external sources, prioritize cybersecurity and ensure compliance with privacy regulations.

Data Fusion Maestro

In this exhilarating journey through working with external data sources, you've transcended the realm of traditional SQL databases. By mastering data import, export, and integration across diverse landscapes, you've earned the title of a data fusion maestro. Your ability to harmonize structured SQL databases with NoSQL, web services, and APIs paints you as a data integration virtuoso, orchestrating symphonies of digital information that propel applications, insights, and innovations to unprecedented heights.

Chapter 11: Real-World Application Scenarios

In the dynamic realm of data-driven applications, the true essence of SQL shines when put into action. This chapter embarks on a journey through real-world application scenarios, demonstrating how SQL transcends theory to deliver tangible solutions. By immersing ourselves in practical use cases, we uncover the magic that SQL weaves into the fabric of modern software engineering.

Building Reports and Dashboards with SQL

Reports and dashboards are the windows through which users gain insights into data. **Building Reports and Dashboards with SQL** is an art that empowers you to translate raw data into meaningful visuals.

Data Extraction: Query databases to retrieve the necessary data for reports. Utilize filtering, aggregation, and joins to assemble comprehensive datasets.

Visualization Platforms: Integrate SQL with visualization tools like Tableau, Power BI, or custom web frameworks to craft engaging visualizations.

Dynamic Filters: Implement dynamic filtering in reports, enabling users to interactively explore data subsets.

Performance Optimization: Optimize SQL queries to ensure swift data retrieval, especially when dealing with large datasets.

Example: Construct a sales dashboard that provides an overview of monthly revenue trends, top-selling products, and regional performance using a combination of SQL queries and visualization tools.

E-Commerce Inventory Management System

In the realm of e-commerce, **inventory management systems** are critical for maintaining stock levels, processing orders, and ensuring seamless customer experiences.

Stock Tracking: Utilize SQL to track inventory levels, implementing alerts for low-stock items.

Order Processing: Integrate SQL with order management systems to ensure accurate order fulfillment and minimize discrepancies.

Dynamic Pricing: Leverage historical sales data and real-time market trends to implement dynamic pricing strategies.

Example: Develop an inventory management system that optimizes stock replenishment, minimizes stockouts, and provides insights into sales patterns and product performance.

Healthcare Patient Records System

The healthcare industry relies heavily on accurate and accessible patient records. An effective **patient records system** can revolutionize patient care and administrative efficiency.

Data Normalization: Design databases that maintain data integrity by adhering to normalization principles, reducing data redundancy.

Data Privacy: Implement security measures to ensure patient data confidentiality and compliance with privacy regulations.

Query Performance: Optimize SQL queries for quick access to patient records during diagnosis and treatment.

Example: Create a patient records system that allows healthcare professionals to easily access and update patient information, schedule appointments, and review medical histories.

Educational Institution Management System

In the education sector, managing student data, course offerings, and academic progress is paramount.

Course Scheduling: Use SQL to design efficient course scheduling algorithms, avoiding scheduling conflicts.

Student Progress Tracking: Implement SQL-based progress tracking to monitor student performance, grades, and academic milestones.

Communication Hub: Develop a system that connects teachers, students, and parents, facilitating seamless communication.

Example: Construct an educational institution management system that enables efficient enrollment, course registration, grade tracking, and communication among stakeholders.

Elevating Solutions with SQL Prowess

In each of these real-world scenarios, SQL emerges as a powerful enabler, turning theoretical concepts into practical solutions. As you apply your SQL prowess to diverse domains, you bridge the gap between data and meaningful outcomes, creating systems that empower industries and elevate user experiences. The culmination of your SQL expertise lies in your ability to transform raw data into impactful tools that fuel innovation, efficiency, and progress across a multitude of sectors.

Applying SQL to Marketing and Customer Analysis

In the modern business landscape, **marketing and customer analysis** have evolved into data-driven disciplines that fuel strategic decision-making. SQL, with its data manipulation and querying capabilities, emerges as a robust tool for extracting actionable insights from vast customer datasets. Let's explore how SQL empowers marketers to unlock valuable perspectives within their data.

Customer Segmentation

Segmentation lies at the heart of effective marketing. SQL enables the creation of distinct customer segments based on various attributes and behaviors.

Querying with Precision: SQL's SELECT statement allows marketers to filter, group, and sort customer data, enabling dynamic segmentation.

Personalization Potential: By segmenting customers, marketers can craft personalized messages, recommendations, and offers, enhancing engagement.

Behavioral Insights: Analyzing transaction history and interactions, SQL-derived segments uncover behavioral patterns that guide targeted marketing strategies.

Campaign Effectiveness Assessment

Measuring the impact of marketing campaigns is essential for refining strategies. SQL facilitates comprehensive analysis of campaign performance.

Multi-Channel Attribution: SQL's JOIN capabilities assist in attributing conversions to specific campaigns, channels, or touchpoints, providing a holistic view of the customer journey.

A/B Testing Analysis: SQL empowers marketers to compare metrics between different campaign versions, ensuring data-driven decision-making.

Conversion Funnel Understanding: Through SQL-based queries, marketers gain insights into conversion rates at each funnel stage, pinpointing areas for improvement.

Churn Prediction and Retention Strategies

Anticipating and minimizing customer churn is a critical goal. SQL-driven churn prediction informs proactive retention strategies.

Historical Analysis: SQL queries examine historical interactions, enabling the identification of behavior patterns preceding churn events.

Feature Engineering: SQL aids in transforming raw data into predictive features, which machine learning models utilize to forecast churn probabilities.

Data-Driven Interventions: Armed with SQL-derived insights, businesses can deploy targeted interventions to retain at-risk customers.

Customer Lifetime Value Analysis

Understanding the long-term value of customers guides resource allocation and relationship management. SQL calculates and illuminates customer lifetime value (CLV).

SQL Aggregations: SUM, AVG, and other SQL functions provide the means to aggregate purchase data over time for CLV computation.

Segment-Specific Insights: SQL queries facilitate CLV comparison across different segments, informing strategies tailored to various customer groups.

Strategic Alignment: Informed by CLV insights, businesses align their strategies to focus on nurturing and retaining high-value customers.

Seizing Marketing Opportunities with SQL

As marketing evolves into a data-centric realm, SQL plays a pivotal role in extracting meaningful insights from customer data. From segmentation and campaign assessment to churn prediction and CLV analysis, SQL empowers marketers to make informed decisions, optimize strategies, and foster customer-centric growth. By harnessing the power of SQL in marketing and customer analysis, businesses position themselves to thrive in an era where data-driven excellence is the cornerstone of success.

Chapter 12: Future Trends in SQL Programming

Exploring New SQL Features and Enhancements

The world of SQL continues to evolve with an array of new features and enhancements that enrich the querying experience and expand the possibilities of data manipulation. This subsection delves into the exciting terrain of the latest advancements in SQL, showcasing how they empower engineers and analysts to tackle complex challenges with finesse.

Window Functions: Unleashing Analytical Power

Window functions have revolutionized data analysis within SQL. Their ability to perform calculations across a set of rows related to the current row offers unprecedented analytical depth.

Analytical Insights: Window functions facilitate complex calculations like running totals, rank assignments, and moving averages, providing profound insights.

Data Partitioning: By partitioning data into logical groups, window functions enable context-aware analysis within specific subsets.

Versatility in Use Cases: From financial analysis to time series manipulation, window functions elevate SQL's analytical capabilities to new heights.

Common Table Expressions (CTEs): Enhanced Readability

Common Table Expressions (CTEs) streamline complex queries, enhancing readability and maintainability.

Recursive Queries: CTEs support recursive queries, enabling the exploration of hierarchical data structures like organizational charts.

Subquery Simplification: Replace cumbersome subqueries with CTEs, making queries more comprehensible and modifiable.

Performance Optimization: In certain cases, CTEs can enhance query performance by materializing intermediate results.

JSON Functions: Handling Unstructured Data

As unstructured data gains prominence, SQL's JSON functions offer tools to manipulate and analyze JSON data.

Data Extraction: JSON functions facilitate extraction of specific data points from JSON documents.

Aggregation and Filtering: JSON functions enable aggregation and filtering within JSON arrays and objects.

Integration with Applications: JSON functions ease interaction with JSON-based APIs and external services.

Temporal Data: Navigating Time Travel

SQL's temporal data capabilities empower users to navigate time-based changes in data.

Valid Time and Transaction Time: Temporal tables allow users to query data at specific points in time or track historical changes over time.

Auditing and Compliance: Temporal data features facilitate compliance with audit and regulatory requirements.

Analyzing Historical Trends: Temporal queries enable retrospective analysis of data changes and trends.

Machine Learning Integration: Bridging SQL and AI

The fusion of SQL and machine learning unleashes the potential to perform data analysis and predictions within a single platform.

Predictive Insights: SQL's integration with machine learning models facilitates predictive analytics directly within the database.

Data Preparation: Use SQL to preprocess and transform data before feeding it to machine learning algorithms.

Scalability and Efficiency: By processing data and AI tasks in the same environment, efficiency and scalability are enhanced.

Embracing the SQL Frontier

The world of SQL continually evolves, incorporating advancements that empower professionals to push boundaries and solve complex challenges. Window functions for analytical depth, CTEs for enhanced readability, JSON functions for unstructured data, temporal data capabilities for time-based analysis, and the fusion of SQL with machine learning exemplify the innovations that propel SQL's capabilities to new horizons.

By staying abreast of these features, SQL enthusiasts harness a potent toolkit to tackle diverse data scenarios with flair and finesse.

Integration with Machine Learning and AI: Unleashing Data Superpowers

In the era of data-driven innovation, the fusion of SQL with Machine Learning and Artificial Intelligence (AI) emerges as a transformative force. This subsection embarks on an exhilarating journey through the realm where structured querying meets the realm of predictive analytics, opening doors to powerful insights and possibilities.

A Glimpse of the Future: Predictive Analytics with SQL

Imagine leveraging the power of SQL not just for querying, but also for predicting future outcomes. This is where SQL's integration with machine learning shines.

Example: Customer Churn Prediction

Suppose you're in charge of a subscription-based service. By combining SQL's analytical capabilities with machine learning algorithms, you can predict which customers are likely to churn. This proactive insight empowers you to implement targeted retention strategies, reducing churn and enhancing customer satisfaction.

From Raw Data to AI-Ready: Data Preprocessing

AI thrives on quality data. SQL plays a pivotal role in preparing raw data for machine learning algorithms.

Example: Sentiment Analysis

Imagine you're building a sentiment analysis model for customer reviews. SQL's data transformation abilities can help you clean, preprocess, and organize textual data into a format that AI algorithms can digest. Your SQL-powered preprocessing paves the way for more accurate sentiment predictions.

In-Database Predictions: Streamlined Insights

Performing machine learning predictions within the SQL environment boosts efficiency and streamlines workflows.

Example: Fraud Detection

Consider a financial institution aiming to identify fraudulent transactions. By integrating machine learning models directly into SQL, the institution can swiftly analyze transaction patterns and predict potential fraud, all within the same database environment.

Scalability and Beyond: SQL + AI Collaboration

The collaboration between SQL and AI transcends mere analysis; it's about enabling innovations at scale.

Example: Recommender Systems

Think of an e-commerce platform aiming to offer personalized product recommendations to users. SQL, in tandem with AI algorithms, can analyze user behavior, historical purchases, and preferences to generate tailor-made recommendations that keep customers engaged and increase sales.

Mastering the Fusion for Data Superpowers

The integration of SQL with Machine Learning and AI is not just about data analysis; it's about data superpowers. By tapping into this fusion, you're not only querying your data; you're predicting future trends, optimizing strategies, and unleashing the potential to revolutionize industries. From predicting customer behavior to streamlining AI-powered insights, the synergy of SQL and AI propels you into the realm of data-driven excellence, where innovation knows no bounds.

The Evolving Role of SQL in Data-Driven Decision Making

In an age where data is the currency of informed decision making, the role of SQL has evolved from a mere querying tool to a cornerstone of data-driven insights. The marriage of SQL's querying prowess with modern data analysis methodologies has ushered in a new era of strategic decision making. In this section, we embark on a journey through the transformation of SQL's role in data-driven decision making, exploring its integration with advanced analytics, its relevance in diverse industries, and real-world code examples that illuminate its impact.

From Querying to Insight: SQL's Evolution

Traditionally, SQL was synonymous with querying structured databases. Today, it transcends mere querying, acting as a gateway to extracting actionable insights from intricate datasets.

Example: Retail Analytics

Consider a retail business analyzing sales trends. While SQL can retrieve historical sales data, its evolution involves utilizing analytical functions to calculate moving averages, identify sales peaks, and forecast demand patterns. This elevates SQL from a querying tool to an analytical powerhouse.

SQL Meets Advanced Analytics: The Synergy

The integration of SQL with advanced analytics techniques enriches its role in decision making.

Example: Customer Segmentation

Let's say you're managing an e-commerce platform. By employing SQL's GROUP BY and analytics functions, you can segment customers based on their purchasing behavior, enabling targeted marketing campaigns. The fusion of SQL's querying capabilities with data science techniques transforms data into strategic insights.

SQL Copy code

```sql
SELECT CASE
    WHEN total_spent >= 1000 THEN 'High Value'
    WHEN total_spent >= 500 THEN 'Medium Value'
    ELSE 'Low Value'
END AS customer_segment,
COUNT(*) AS segment_count
FROM customers
GROUP BY customer_segment;
```

SQL's Ubiquity Across Industries

The evolution of SQL's role isn't confined to specific sectors. Its influence permeates industries, driving decisions across the board.

Example: Healthcare Analytics

In the healthcare sector, SQL plays a pivotal role in analyzing patient data. You can employ SQL to calculate average patient wait times, assess hospital resource utilization, and identify trends in patient admissions. This aids hospitals in optimizing patient care and resource allocation.

SQL Copy code

```
SELECT AVG(wait_time_minutes) AS avg_wait_time, department
FROM patient_records
GROUP BY department;
```

Decision-Driving Power: SQL and Real-Time Analytics

The dynamic nature of real-time analytics merges seamlessly with SQL's capabilities, enabling swift decision making.

Example: Stock Market Analysis

For financial analysts, real-time data is essential. SQL can be used to analyze stock market data in real time, identifying trends, anomalies, and predicting market movements.

SQL Copy code

```
SELECT stock_symbol, MAX(price) AS highest_price, MIN(price) AS lowest_price, AVG(volume) AS avg_volume
FROM stock_market_data
WHERE date >= NOW() - INTERVAL 1 DAY
GROUP BY stock_symbol;
```

SQL for All: Democratizing Data Insights

SQL's user-friendly syntax and wide adoption democratize data insights, enabling professionals from diverse backgrounds to make informed decisions.

Example: Marketing Metrics

Imagine a marketing professional analyzing campaign performance. SQL empowers them to query data, calculate conversion rates, and assess the Return on Investment (ROI) of different marketing initiatives.

SQL Copy code

```sql
SELECT campaign_name,
       SUM(conversions) AS total_conversions,
       SUM(spend) AS total_spend,
       SUM(conversions) / SUM(spend) AS ROI
FROM marketing_data
GROUP BY campaign_name;
```

SQL's Renaissance in Decision Making

The evolution of SQL in data-driven decision making is a renaissance, marked by its transformation from a querying tool to a strategic asset. From its integration with advanced analytics to its relevance across industries, SQL's journey encapsulates its enduring significance. The real-world code examples showcased here illustrate the practical application of SQL in diverse scenarios, proving its role in fostering strategic insights and driving business excellence.

As we navigate the data-driven future, SQL stands as a beacon, guiding professionals towards a landscape where decisions are not just informed, but empowered by data-driven precision.

Conclusion

Navigating Your SQL Odyssey

As we draw the final curtain on this SQL journey, take a moment to reflect on the remarkable voyage you've undertaken. From your first encounter with SQL's SELECT statement to crafting intricate queries that unveil profound insights, you've traversed a landscape where data meets ingenuity. The pages of this book have been your compass, guiding you through the intricate terrain of SQL programming, data manipulation, and advanced analysis.

Reflecting on Your SQL Journey

Remember the first time you executed a basic query, eagerly awaiting the results that materialized before your eyes? Those humble beginnings have led you to comprehend complex joins, wield window functions, and integrate machine learning into your SQL toolkit. You've learned to translate business challenges into elegant SQL solutions, transforming raw data into actionable wisdom.

As you reflect on your SQL journey, embrace the evolution you've undergone. The once-novel commands are now familiar tools you employ to navigate the world of data.

Each chapter has contributed to the transformation of your SQL skills, refining your ability to extract value from data and drive informed decision making.

Encouragement to Continue Exploring and Learning SQL

Your journey doesn't end here; it evolves. SQL is a dynamic realm, continually adapting to technological advancements and expanding horizons. As you close this chapter, remember that learning is a perpetual process. The universe of SQL is vast, and there's always more to explore.

Continue to challenge yourself with complex queries, experiment with new features, and push the boundaries of your SQL expertise. Delve into topics like optimization, database administration, and emerging database technologies. Embrace opportunities to collaborate with fellow enthusiasts, as the synergy of shared knowledge propels growth.

Your journey is a testament to your dedication, curiosity, and eagerness to embrace the transformative power of SQL. You've equipped yourself with a toolset that empowers you to contribute meaningfully in a data-driven world. So, step forward with confidence, knowing that your SQL odyssey is not just a chapter in your story but a foundation for a future fueled by data-driven excellence.

🚀 **Your SQL journey is only the beginning. Happy querying and exploring!** 🚀

Appendix: Additional Resources

Recommended Books, Online Courses, and Tutorials

Delve deeper into the world of SQL with these recommended resources:

- **"SQL Performance Explained"** by Markus Winand: A comprehensive guide to understanding and optimizing SQL performance.

- **"SQL For Smarties"** by Joe Celko: A classic text exploring advanced SQL concepts and techniques.

- **Coursera**: Offers a variety of SQL courses from universities and institutions worldwide.

- **edX**: Features SQL courses from renowned universities and organizations.

- **Udemy**: Provides a plethora of SQL courses catering to different skill levels.

- **Khan Academy**: Offers free SQL tutorials suitable for beginners.

SQL Cheat Sheets and Quick References

Keep these cheat sheets and references handy for quick access to SQL commands and syntax:

- **W3Schools SQL Cheat Sheet**: A concise reference for SQL syntax and common commands.

- **SQLZoo Cheat Sheet**: A visual guide to basic SQL commands and concepts.

- **SQL Quick Reference Guide**: A comprehensive overview of SQL commands and functions.

Online Communities and Forums for SQL Enthusiasts

Join these communities to connect with fellow SQL enthusiasts, ask questions, and share your knowledge:

- **Stack Overflow**: A vibrant community where you can ask SQL-related questions and get answers from experts.

- **SQLServerCentral**: A forum dedicated to SQL Server-related discussions and problem-solving.

- **Reddit r/SQL**: Engage in discussions, share insights, and learn from other SQL enthusiasts.

- **Database Administrators Stack Exchange**: A platform for database administrators to exchange knowledge and solve challenges.

Remember that the journey of mastering SQL is a collaborative one. Engaging with these resources and communities will expand your understanding, offer fresh perspectives, and keep you at the forefront of SQL expertise. Happy learning! 🗄️ 💡